I0420811

FITZPATRICK'S

Real Estate

DICTIONARY

Authored by Joseph R. Fitzpatrick

First Edition 2015 08315JF
ISBN-13: 978-1517329242
ISBN-10: 1517329248

1

Joe Fitzpatrick is one of the nation's most predominant real estate instructors and authors with more than twenty published real estate textbooks. This "Real Estate Dictionary" contains more than 500 real estate terms to help you better understand the real estate industry. If you are a licensing candidate, it is our hope that this dictionary will assist you in your licensing efforts.

Joe Fitzpatrick graduated from The University of Nevada, Las Vegas (UNLV) and began his career with Coldwell

Banker Real Estate. There, he managed the North Miami office and eventually opened Century 21 Fitzpatrick Realty with family. The firm became the top-ranked Century 21 company in Broward County. In 1991, Mr. Fitzpatrick returned to Las Vegas where he began teaching and authoring real estate courses. He also continued on as Vice-President of Century 21 MoneyWorld, which was among the top 10 of Century 21 firms in the world, and led the education division among other duties. Mr. Fitzpatrick joined Real Estate School of Nevada as the Director and currently serves as the Vice President of Education for both Real Estate School of Nevada and RealtySchool.com. He has authored and published over twenty real estate licensing textbooks and courses that have been approved and are being utilized in several states.

1031 tax deferred exchanges allows investors to *exchange or trade* their property for other U.S. investment property and may be able to do so without having a current taxable event

abandonment may have occurred if the broker failed to actively market the property. This is really a revocation by the seller with the reason (none actually being required) being the broker has ceased to represent the property.

absentee owners live elsewhere from the subject property

abstract of title summarizes everything found in the public records which will include *recorded* encumbrances and liens. *Unrecorded* matters will not be noted as they will not be found.

acceleration clause allows the lender to call all payments due if the borrower defaults. This allows for a foreclosure of the entire outstanding balance. This clause "accelerates" the time for which payment is due to *now*.

acceptance of offer occurs when all parties agree to every detail of the last offer as submitted, no matter how small

accession refers to trade fixtures not removed by the tenant at the end of a commercial lease becoming the property of the landlord. This term also applies to the accretion of alluvial deposits.

accounting or accountability refers to the agent's receipt of money, property, or other things of value which belong to the client. The agent must account to the client for these items and must use great care in protecting the client's interests.

accretion is the increases in land due to where the action of water has added to the land

acknowledged means to be witnessed by a notary public

acre equals 43,560 square feet

actual eviction is the legal manner in which a landlord evicts the tenant

actual notice is accomplished by **recording** an interest with the county recorder's office. Recording puts the world at large of a recorded interest.

ad valorem tax is a tax levied based upon the property value

addendum is used If the parties discover a need to change or add terms after a contract has been signed

adjustable rate mortgage (ARM) has interest rates that fluctuate with the lender's cost of funds. The ARM has the following elements: index, margin, interval, cap, ceiling and floor, and sometimes a conversion feature.

adjusted basis is the original purchase price of an investment property plus any capital improvements made, less any depreciation previously taken

adjusted gross income, or **effective gross income,** is the income *actually collected or earned*. It is the gross scheduled income less the vacancies and bad debts.

administrator is a court-appointed individual who will oversee the distribution of a deceased's assets if there is no will

agency coupled with an interest refers to the agent having some legal right to, or an interest in, the property that is covered by the agency arrangement. If the agency is coupled with an interest, the agency usually cannot be revoked by the principal before the expiration of the interest. The interest gives the agent a level of legal power over any decisions about the principal's property.

agency describes the fiduciary relationship between the agent and the principal

agricultural real estate involves lands used for farming and cultivating crops, usually 10 or more acres

alienation clause (sometimes referred to as a *due on sale clause)* informs the borrower, in advance, that the lender will not permit an assignment of the borrower's obligations under the note, or interest in the property, unless the lender is paid in full.   As the name implies, the loan is due on sale – if there is a sale, the loan is due. *Alienation* refers to alienating oneself from the property.

alienation refers to "alienating" or separating one's self from the property. The most common example is deeding the property away after a sale has consummated.

all-inclusive deed of trust (or *wrap around mortgage*) is a form of seller financing (purchase money mortgage) available only where there is no existing *due on sale* clause in the original mortgage document. The seller still owes on the original mortgage (the *underlying mortgage*) and continues to make those payments. The buyer makes payments to the seller for the new amount financed as a purchase money mortgage.

allocation of customers occurs when several firms agree to divide markets and refrain from competing for customers. Brokers by internal policy may, however, allocate customers or markets into geographic areas where they plan to operate exclusively.

ALTA title insurance policy is a policy written to the standards of the American Land Title Association.

amenities are other factors that contribute to the subject property's value, in some instances, such as curb appeal, condition of exterior, nearby parks and shops, neighborhood condition, traffic or noise, and the school district.

Americans with Disabilities Act (ADA) is an anti-discrimination law that deals with physical workplace accommodations for disabled persons. The ADA prohibits discrimination in employment practices against persons with disabilities.

amortization is the pattern in which the principal of a loan is paid. With a level payment, fully amortizing loan, the amount of the payment remains the same over the life of the loan, however the components of principal and interest change with each payment. As the balance of the loan is reduced by payment of the principal, the amount for interest will decrease with each payment. This process causes the loan to pay off at the stated term.

annexation refers to converting personal property to real property through the method attachment

annual percentage rate (APR) is the finance charges to obtain the loan, expressed a percentage when applied to the unpaid balance of the loan

anticipation of change may be taking place in some parts of a community. The available uses for parcels may be changing. Local economic considerations may be affecting values. Anticipation of these changes can affect market value.

appraisal is the art of estimating a property's market value. It is an estimate by an appraiser of the current price which will most probably be paid in a market consisting of informed buyers and sellers who are acting under normal and rational motivations. Such a transaction should be at *arm's length*, meaning there is no special pricing because of the relationship of the parties.

appraiser is an individual licensed or certified by a state authority who is educated in the field of valuation and is skilled in estimating the current value of property

appreciation is the increase in value

arm's length means there is no special pricing because of the relationship of the parties; the parties are at an arm's length distance from one another and negotiating in their own best interests

as is is used in many listings to communicate the fact that a property is being sold in its "known" present condition. It does not mean that a seller has been absolved of all responsibility relative to defects of which he or she is aware.

asbestos is found in insulation and in ceiling and floor tiles. Removal is very expensive, and inhalation of asbestos can lead to serious, often fatal lung disease.

assemblage and plottage comes into play when two or more parcels are legally combined into one (assemblage) and the resulting value is higher than the sum of the value of the individual parcels (plottage)

assessed value is the value derived after applying the

assessment ratio to the *market value*.

assessment is the levying of a tax

assessment ratio is an *artificial lowering* of the market value. The assessment ration is applied to the **market value** to determine the **assessed value.**

assigned agency, also called **designated agency,** is utilized in some states where brokers are allowed to "designate" agents to represent clients. This could happen when one salesperson is designated to represent the seller and another is designated to represent the buyer in the same transaction.

assignment clause gives the borrower notice that the lender will likely be transferring the mortgage or deed of trust to another party sometime after the closing on the loan. As a mortgage or deed of trust is a contact, the lender wants to be sure there is no problem with the borrower if the lender assigns the contract to another investor or to the **Secondary Mortgage Market**.

assignment of contract may occur when one party desires to assign his rights, obligations, and benefits under the contract to a third party. However that original party will remain liable for performance and obligations should the third party fail to perform. This is called **secondary liability**. Contracts are freely and fully assignable unless prohibited in the agreement.

assumption clause describes under what circumstances, if any, the lender will allow another person to assume the mortgage or deed of trust

assumption of a mortgage means a person is acquiring property with an underlying loan and agrees to personally take over financial responsibility for the mortgage.

attestation in a deed is the notary public's swearing that the signing parties appeared before the notary, swore they were who they said they were, were authorized to sign the deed and did so as their free act, and actually signed the deed in the presence of the notary public

avulsion is the sudden removal of soil by an act of nature can cause a landowner's property to become much smaller very quickly

balloon loan amortizes at the stated interest rate and term, as if it were a fully amortizing loan, but requires an early payoff in a lump sum

bargain and sale deed contains an implied warranty of seisin. There are no written warranties and is only an implication that the grantor has title and the legal right to convey it.

base lines are the primary horizontal lines referenced when using the U.S. Government Rectangular Survey system

benchmark is a permanent reference mark, sometimes called a "brass cap," usually embedded in streets or sidewalks and used by surveyors as a reference point for elevations

beneficiary is the lender in a deed of trust

bequest is personal property given through a will

bilateral contracts are two-sided agreements where both parties are making promises and are undertaking performing those promises. One promise is given in exchange for another.

blanket mortgage will cover multiple parcels and is common in subdivision development financing. This loan will have a *partial release clause* allowing the builder to pull the parcel sold "out from under" the blanket mortgage.

blockbusting is the illegal attempting to create panic selling by creating a sales contract with a member of a protected class with the intent to use the sale to a protected class member as a method of inducing owners in the area to sell, before the neighborhood becomes too "mixed" or the homes lose value

boot is money or property added to make up the difference in value between two properties being exchanged in a 1031 deferred exchange

breach of contract occurs if either of the parties to a contract fails or refuses to perform any duties per the contract. The injured party has legal remedies available.

broker is an agent who agrees to represent the interests of the principal, and who agrees to let the broker exercise authority on behalf of the principal

broker price opinion is a tool to determine value as requested by a third party such as the lender in the case of foreclosure and by a relocation company in the event of an executive transfer that will result in a buyout. "BPOs" are generally performed by licensed real estate agents and brokers for a nominal fee. BPOs are normally more involved than a market analysis and less sophisticated than an appraisal.

brokerage is the matchmaking of people and bringing them together in a transaction of some kind

budget loans have payments of principal, interest, taxes, and insurance (PITI) and the mortgage insurance premium is included in the monthly payment

buffer zones are required separations between conflicting uses. They are often an area of land zoned for a use that smoothly *transitions* from one use to another.

building codes are enforced by requiring the builder to submit plans before construction can be commenced, and once the plans are approved, periodic inspections are conducted to be sure the construction is following the approved plans and is being done in a workman like manner

building permit has to be issued before construction can be commenced by the developer

bundle of rights include possession, control, enjoyment, exclusion, and disposition

business opportunities involves the sale or lease of existing businesses

buydown results when discount points are paid to buy the interest rate down and hence the name "discount" points

buyer brokerage agreement establishes an exclusive relationship where the buyer employs the broker to locate the desired property and to negotiate with the sellers on the buyer's behalf for the best available price and terms for a purchase (or a lease if a tenant representation agreement)

cap refers to the maximum the interest rate can change in any interval. This will be stated in the note and will not be changed for the life of the loan.

capital gain occurs when an asset is sold for more than its original cost basis. The *profit* realized may represent a capital gain. If the property is an investment property, the capital gain can probably be treated under the capital gain provisions in the tax code.

capital improvement is a major or significant improvement to investment property which will add value to the investment property and is of a durable nature and which will or is expected to last several years

capitalization rate, cap rate, desired rate of return, or ***return on investment***, is the yield to the investor for investing in the income property. This rate may be determined based on the current income and value of the property, or the rate the investor demands. This rate will be compared to alternate investments such as stocks, bonds, mutual funds, and anything the investor may have an interest in.

capitalization refers to estimating the value of property by dividing the net operating income by a desired rate of return (capitalization rate)

carbon monoxide (CO) is a colorless and odorless gas that occurs as a byproduct of burning certain types of fuels. It can pose a significant health hazard if not properly ventilated.

caveat emptor, translating to "buyer beware," refers to the buyer's obligation to discover all of the possible things wrong with a property before the purchase is consummated

ceiling and floor, sometimes called the ***lifetime cap,*** the ceiling represents the maximum interest rate the borrower can be charged anytime during the life of the loan. Likewise, the ***floor*** represents the minimum interest rate the borrower will have to pay anytime during the life of the loan. This will be stated in the note and will not be changed for the life of the loan.

certificate of reasonable value (CRV) is the VA appraisal

chain of title is a history report making sure the title company can "link" each owner from the current owner all the way back to the first owner with no gaps (breaks) in the links

change and anticipation of change may be taking place in some parts of a community. The available uses for parcels may be changing. Local economic considerations may be affecting values.

chattel is another word for personal property

Civil Rights Act of 1866 (Reconstruction Act) provides that all persons born in the United States are declared to be citizens, regardless of race or color, and shall have the right to enter into contracts, to sue, inherit, acquire and dispose of property, and shall equally benefit from the law as do white citizens. Classes protected by this law are race and color.

client is the principal to whom the agent is expected to give advice and counsel during the period of agency

CLTA title insurance policy is a title policy written to the standards of the California Land Title Association

Code of Ethics and Standards of Practice are the rules by which all members of the National Association of REALTORS® agree to abide

codicil is a modification to a will

collateral is the real or personal property upon which the lien is given to secure the borrowing

commercial real estate involves income producing properties such as multi-unit dwellings, retail shopping centers, office buildings, etc.

common elements are components of the property, usually condominiums, that all owners benefit from and enjoy such as the club house, swimming pool, and other amenities.

These are owned by all (**undivided interest**) of the condominium owners as *tenants in common.*

common interest communities (CICs) are often organized by a new home builder and set standards of behavior and living for a defined community. This is done through the establishment of **conditions, covenants & restrictions (CC&Rs)** that all homeowners agree to follow.

community property statutes create the possibility that a married couple may have property which belongs solely to the wife, or solely to the husband, or property which is held by them as community property. Community property is all property acquired by either the husband or the wife during the marriage and each spouse is presumed to own a 50% interest in the community property.

comparable sales approach or **market data approach** is the most common particularly for residential properties. The appraiser looks for properties which have sold recently, in close proximity, and comparable in features and amenities to the subject property.

comparables are recently sold properties that resemble the subject property but are not identical, and therefore some adjustments may be required

comparative market analysis (CMA) CMA is often prepared by a real estate agent when listing property for sale and may show current, available listings for sale, pending sales, closed sales, withdrawn listings, and expired listings

competent parties means all parties must be living, of lawful age, of sound mind, and mentally competent

Comprehensive Environmental Response, Compensation, and Liability Act (1980), CERCLA, established a *Superfund* to clean up hazardous waste sites and to collect the costs from certain responsible persons associated with the sites

condemnation is the process of *taking the property* under ***eminent domain***, while the *payment for the property* is normally referred to as a ***condemnation award***

conditional commitment is the FHA appraisal

conditional use permit (CUP) **could grant a use in an area where there is** not a specific zone in which it could otherwise be put. This often applies to a use, such as a hospital placed in a residential zone, for the betterment of the community.

conditions, covenants and restrictions (CC&Rs) placed by the developer of a restricted community creating certain conditions and restrictions on the property, including the creation of a Common Interest Community (CIC). These restrictions bind all future owners. The restrictions are usually managed by a homeowners' association (HOA), which often hires a property management company to enforce the restrictions.

condominium is, in reality, *a space in the building*, and the condo owner has ownership of only the internal walls, cabinets, fixtures, appliances, carpets, floors, etc.

confidentiality, as it pertains to the fiduciary duties, refers to the agent's obligation to keep confidential all information about the client which, if disclosed without the principal's permission, could hurt the principal's bargaining position

conformity refers to how consistent the subject property is with the other surrounding properties. If a property is significantly better than surrounding properties, its value will *regress* downward toward the value of the surrounding properties. If a property is significantly poorer than surrounding properties, the surrounding properties will tend to cause the subject property's value to *progress* upward as a result of the higher value of the surrounding properties.

consideration clause will be found in a deed reflecting one of these four types of consideration (anything of value) being offered

consideration may be money, anything of value, or just a statement that consideration exists, such as "for continued love and affection" or "for good and valuable consideration"

construction loan is a loan for construction purposes, usually a short term loan, two to five years depending on the length of time required, to build the project. It is considered **interim financing** until the builder can secure permanent financing to complete the project. The developer makes periodic *draws* against the maximum loan amount as construction progresses. The lender normally inspects each phase of construction to assure there is enough construction to serve as collateral. Normally the funds can only be used for construction of the project which is the collateral for the construction mortgage. This is considered a riskier loan and is priced accordingly. These are usually interest-only loans.

constructive eviction means the landlord has done, or failed to do, something that has had the effect of denying the tenant the use and enjoyment of the leasehold. Often this involves matters of landlord maintenance which has not been done. Changing the locks is a common scenario of an unlawful constructive eviction.

constructive notice is a legal principle that a party was actually given notice of an interest

Consumer Credit Protection Act, Truth-In-Lending Act, Regulation "Z" provide the consumer with complete and understandable credit information so the consumer can make informed credit decisions. The disclosures required by these laws are finance charges and the disclosure of the annual percentage rate.

contingency is a clause written into a contract stating some event must be completed before all of the duties of the contract can be or will be performed. Contingencies include new loan approval, sale of current residence, inspections to be conducted, etc. If the contingency is not fulfilled or waived, the contract is voidable.

contract for deed is a form of seller financing. In the contract for deed, sometimes called a **Land Contract**, the **vendor** (seller) retains *legal title* to the property but transfers e*quitable title* to the **vendee** (buyer). If the buyer does perform as required, then at the conclusion of performance, the seller is obligated to convey legal title to the buyer where it will join with the equitable title the buyer already holds.

contract is a voluntary agreement between informed and capable parties to do, or to refrain from doing, something which is legal to do, and which is supported by adequate consideration

contribution is what the market will pay for a feature or amenity. The value the feature or amenity *contributes* is not necessarily equal to its cost.

conventional loan is a loan that is neither FHA nor VA; made with *neither* federal government insurance nor guarantees

conversion gives the borrower the option of *converting* to a fixed rate mortgage at various periods during the loan. Usually, these are at 3 years, 5 years, and 7 years.

cooperating brokers refer to buyer brokers who work with (cooperate with) listing brokers to produce a buyer who is ready, willing, and able to purchase

cooperative apartments were created in major cities on the eastern seaboard when developers and investors realized that apartment and other buildings with residential potential would be far more profitable if the units could be sold rather than rented. The concept was created to form a corporation, which would own the building and sell shares of stock in the building, each share of stock entitling the owner to a **proprietary lease**.

corporation is a *legal person* meaning it can sue and be sued in court. A corporation consists of one or more shareholders who own stock in the corporation.

cost approach determines what it would cost to replace the subject property as if it were being built from the land up. Using informational sources available to the appraiser, the subject property is "rebuilt" on paper.

counteroffer is *any change,* no matter how small or large, made to the offer. A counteroffer rejects the offer as written, but modifies what terms and conditions must be changed to make the offer acceptable.

covenant (or **warranty)** is a promise by the grantor to the grantee concerning the title to the property, that some condition exists and will continue to exist, or, that a condition does not exist and never will.

curable depreciation/obsolescence has two (2) elements: that the depreciation can be cured (fixed or repaired), and that the added value to the property by curing the depreciation will be more than the cost to cure it *curtesy* is a husband's legal interest, upon his wife's death, to property his wife has or acquired during their marriage

custom homes are where the builder has a buyer under contract to build a specific home that was designed and blueprinted by an architect

customer is a third party for whom a service is provided by the agent, but to whom the agent owes no fiduciary duties

datum is a permanent reference mark used by surveyors as a reference point for elevations

dedication is the act of turning over ownership to subdivision amenities such as streets, sidewalks, and green areas

deed is the only instrument used for the conveyance of title to land

deed of trust is a contract which creates a *monetary lien* against real property. Deeds of trust are most frequently used in the states west of the Rocky Mountains. In a deed of trust, there are three parties: the *trustor* (the borrower), the *trustee* (an independent third party chosen by the lender), and the *beneficiary* (the lender).

deed restrictions put certain restrictions on the future use of the property by including these limitations in the deed

defeasance clause requires the lender to issue a *satisfaction of mortgage* indicating the loan has been paid in full

defeasible fee (or *fee simple defeasible* or *determinable fee*), has an attached stipulation such as "for as long as" or "during" and provided that condition is not broken, the holder remains in title. Upon the occurrence of that designated event, title to the property **reverts** back to the former grantor.

deficiency judgment may be sought by the lender should the proceeds from a foreclosure sale or short sale, be insufficient to satisfy the loan

demand suggests that of the market does not want the property, it has little or no value. **Effective Demand** refers to the market having the capacity or ability to purchase the property. If the market lacks adequate purchasing power to buy the property, the property's value is greatly diminished.

depreciation is the reduction in value as a result of age, poor state of repair, poor design, etc. It is the loss in value for any reason. Buildings and improvements depreciate; land does not.

designated agency is another term for assigned agency

devise is real property given to a **devisee** through a will

disclosure is the agent's duty to keep the client informed (to disclose) of all material facts which may have any importance in matters where the agent is representing the client

discount point equals 1% of the loan amount. The IRS considers a point to be a form of interest paid upfront instead of over the term of the loan. Discount points are charged when there is a cost to receive a certain rate or to buy a rate down ("discount").

discount rate is the interest rate the Federal Reserve System charges its member banks. If the Federal Reserve Board of Governors feels inflationary pressures in the economy exist, they may decide to raise the discount rate, which would have the effect of making borrowing more expensive for business and consumers and in theory cooling the business economy and reducing inflationary pressure. The converse is also true. If the "Fed" thinks a little boost to the economy is needed, they might decide to reduce the discount rate making borrowing less expensive and encouraging consumers to spend more and for businesses to expand their operations, production and hiring.

dominant tenement enjoys the right to pass over the servient tenement's land

dower is a wife's legal interest, upon her husband's death, to property her husband has or acquired during their marriage

down zoning **has** occurred if uses a property already had are *taken away.* This may reduce the value of the property.

dual agency is a situation where one agent represents both buyer and seller. In some states, dual agency is not allowed. In others, it is allowed, but only with the expressed, informed consent of both represented parties. This is sometimes referred to as **multiple-party representation**.

due diligence is that period of time, as granted in the purchase agreement, for the buyer to perform the inspections necessary to ensure that defects do not exist. For these reasons, many buyers perform a home inspection, a pest inspection, or any other inspections desired during this period. Contracts are usually contingent upon the results of these inspections allowing the buyer to cancel the contract without penalty.

due on sale clause (sometimes referred to as an **alienation clause**) informs the borrower, in advance, that the lender will not permit an assignment of the borrower's obligations under the note, or interest in the property, unless the lender is paid in full. As the name implies, the loan is due on sale – if there is a sale, the loan is due. "Alienation" refers to alienating oneself from the property.

duty of further inquiry is part of the agent's duty to the principal. If the agent acquires information which would cause a reasonable person to ask some questions, the agent is expected to do so.

earnest money deposit is typically money that accompanies an offer to show the buyer's "earnestness" in completing the contract as it is often sacrificed upon a breach of contract

easement appurtenant is between owners of *neighboring* properties giving one owner a right of passage over the other owner's property

easement by necessity may come into play should a person find that he has purchased property which does not have *ingress* (entrance) or *egress* (exit) to the public way. This generally will involve court action and the court will seek to find the least intrusive method to give the landlocked property owner access to the public way.

easement by prescription is seldom seen in modern times, but arise through one party's conspicuous use of a portion of another's property to cross over. The use would have to have been for a "prescribed," long period of time, normally 21 years or longer (the time period varies by state); would have to be without the permission of the landowner; would have to be continuous; and would have to be "hostile" meaning contrary to the rights of the owner of the property being crossed.

easement in gross has only a servient tenement. The most common examples of an easement in gross are *utility easements*.

easement is the right of someone other than the owner to use part of a property for a specific purpose. Easements are typically recorded with the legal description, noted on a plat map, or otherwise part of the property records.

effective gross income, or *adjusted gross income,* is the income *actually collected or earned.* It is the gross scheduled income less the vacancies and bad debts.

egress (exit) to the public way

electromagnetic fields (EMFs) are fields generated by the movement of electrical currents, such as in power transmission lines

electronic contracting is a means by which agents can handle contracts by digital, or electronic methods. The *Uniform Electronic Transaction Act (UETA)* and the *Electronic Signatures in Global and National Commerce Act (E-Sign)* are the two federal laws that govern these activities.

emblements (or *fructus industriales)* include fruit, vegetables, nuts, grasses, grains and other annually cultivated crops. These are considered personal property.

eminent domain means private property can be taken by the government, provided the tests of proof of a public use and payment of just compensation are met
enabling acts allow local governments decision-making authority for the individual circumstances of a community. This is mostly relevant to zoning.

encumbrance is defined as *a burden upon the title to the property,* even though great benefits may be derived by the owner as a result of the encumbrance *enforceable* means a dispute between the parties will be heard in court and a judge will "enforce" the provisions of the contract

environmental impact statement (EIS) identifies the anticipated effects of developing a new project as they pertain to the safety and health of the public

Equal Credit Opportunity Act (ECOA) prohibits creditors from discriminating against credit applicants on the basis of race, color, religion, national origin, sex, marital status, age, or because an applicant receives income from a public assistance program

equalization factor may be applied to adjust for assessors who either tend to be high or low in their assessments

equitable title refers to the buyer's interests in the property while either in escrow or when making payments on a loan where the mortgagee is carrying the financing such as with a contract for deed. *Equitable title* or an *equitable interest* suggests the buyer has the property under contract and no one else does. The rights associated with equitable title vary from state to state.

equity loans, or home equity lines of credit (HELOC), may be done when the homeowner has a substantial amount of equity in the property and wishes to use that equity (by borrowing against it) for some other purpose. These loans are sometimes called *open end mortgages* as the loan is considered "open ended" for future advances from the lender usually to a pre-determined amount.

erosion removes land due to wind, rain, or flowing water and replaced it with water. The missing land no longer belongs to the landowner.

escalation lease is similar to an indexed lease, except that the tenant's lease payment is increased by the actual increases in the operating expenses of the property and not directly tied to an inflation index

escheat describes when a person dies with no will, and after a reasonable search, no heirs are found. The property will pass to the state by escheat.

escrow account is another term for a **trust account** established by a broker for the holding of the principal's funds until funding, such as with a buyer's earnest money deposit

escrow instructions is the escrowee's own document spelling out all the details of the transaction. Many times the purchase agreement also serves as escrow instructions.

escrow refers to the closing process as conducted by a third party called the escrowee

escrowee is an escrow company or agent, such as an attorney, who facilitates the close of escrow

estate at sufferance is the status of the parties where the term of the lease has expired and the tenant remains in possession without the landlord's consent. The tenant has no right to be there and is technically a trespasser. As the name implies, the landlord is "suffering" due to the tenant's continued presence in the property.

estate at will is an open-ended lease with no specific termination date and therefore, notice is required to terminate this lease. Should the parties have failed to specify the length of the notice period, the courts will require a "reasonable" notice be given.

estate for years is a type of lease has a definite starting and ending date. The term can be of any duration. No notice is required to terminate.

estate from period to period is a type of lease which has a stated *period of time* which will automatically renew for the same period over and over again until one party gives notice they no longer wish to continue

eviction is the lawful process of dispossessing a tenant who has either overstayed the lease term, or who is in breach of the lease, and eviction has been elected as a remedy by the landlord

exceptions and reservations clause is where the grantor will make the grant subject to any exceptions, encumbrances, or liens on title which will not be removed by the grantor. This clause is also where the grantor may create restriction or easements.

exclusive agency listing is a form of listing contract whereby the seller agrees to hire the broker on an exclusive basis, and agrees to pay a commission to the exclusive broker when the exclusive broker, or any other broker, produces a ready, willing, and able buyer at list price and terms or such other price and terms agreeable to the seller. The seller gives *exclusivity* to the broker and agrees that all other brokers must go through the exclusive broker. However, the seller may sell the property himself without owing a commission.

exclusive right to sell listing is a form of listing contract whereby the seller agrees to hire the broker on an exclusive basis and agrees to pay a commission to the exclusive broker when the exclusive broker, or any other broker, produces a ready, willing, and able buyer at list price and terms or such other price and terms agreeable to the seller. The seller gives *exclusivity* to the broker and agrees that all other brokers must go through the exclusive broker and further agrees that should the seller find a buyer on his own, he will still owe a commission to the exclusive broker.

executed contract is one that is fully and completely performed. "Executed," in a different context, can also mean that the contract has been fully signed by all parties. *executor* the named individual in a will who will oversee the distribution of a deceased's assets

executory contract is not yet fully performed. For example, a 30 year mortgage is "executory" until the making of the last payment, if not paid off in full sooner. It is not "executed" until it is paid in full.

expressed agency occurs when a formal document is signed, binding the parties to an agency relationship. Once signed, a listing agreement, buyer's brokerage agreement, or similar document, creates an agency relationship. Note that "expressed" also means "using words" which includes verbal contracting.

expressed means the use of words, either written or oral, to show intentions of the parties to the contract

external/environmental/locational/economic obsolescence are four names all for the same thing. The property is located in an "environment" or in a "location" in which the market will penalize the value, such as the subject property being adjacent to a waste facility.

Fair Housing Act, formally known as Title VIII of the Civil Rights Act of 1968, protects four classes or classifications of Americans. Race and color from 1866 and in 1968 covered religion and national origin. Gender was added in 1974 and family status and disability were added in 1988.

farming is prospecting in a geographical area, staying in contact with all residents of a select neighborhood (the *farm*), providing information and real estate services

Federal Home Loan Mortgage Corporation (FHLMC "Freddie Mac") purchases qualified residential mortgages from the originators. Freddie Mac then issues a security to private investors which represents an undivided interest in the mortgages Freddie Mac owns. These securities contain a guarantee against loss to the investor. Freddie Mac deals in residential mortgages which *do not* contain U.S. government backed loans; these are the so called *conventional* mortgages.

Federal National Mortgage Association (FNMA "Fannie Mae") is a major warehouse underwriter of conventional loans as well as U.S. government insured (FHA) or guaranteed loans (VA).

Federal Trade Commission (FTC) is the primary enforcement body for truth-in-advertising claims, although a number of state agencies are also active in this regard. If real estate customers or clients have fallen victim to advertising violations, the law allows for the reporting of a complaint and remediation. Generally, truth-in-advertising laws require print, TV, magazine, newspaper, Internet, and other advertising to be truthful, non-deceptive, provable by evidence furnished by the advertiser, and fair.

fee simple absolute is the highest quality interest in real estate in that the holder has all the rights recognized by law. With an estate in fee simple, the estate runs forever and upon the death of the owner, the property is inheritable to the heirs. This is the ideal form of ownership.

FHA insured loans are loans made by private lenders who make the loan to a qualified borrower and the FHA *insures* the lender against loss on the loan. With the "full faith and credit" of the United States government standing behind the loan, private lenders are willing to make these loans, thereby meeting the needs of the home buying population and stimulating the economy.

fiduciary duties involve "trust and confidence" and are owed by the agent to the principal in the transaction, who may be the buyer, seller, lessor, or lessee of property. The six fiduciary duties are *care, obedience, loyalty, disclosure, accounting, and confidentiality* — often remembered by the acronym COLDAC.

financing is simply the borrowing of money. It may be borrowing from a private party or a professional lender. The borrowing may be unsecured (no collateral, only the credit worthiness of the borrower is considered), or the borrowing may be secured (real or personal property is given to assure repayment of the loan).

fixtures are items of personal property that have been permanently attached to land or a building, so that they become part of the real property

flat fee commissions are established in the listing contract as a specific amount, regardless of what the purchase price turns out to be

Foreign Investor in Real Property Tax Act (FIRPTA) applies to the sale of properties in the United States by foreign nationals or foreign corporations. At close of escrow, 10% of the gross sale price will be withheld and transmitted to the IRS.

fraud involves the intentional misrepresentation of a material fact. Fraud is also the intentional use of deceit, a trick, or some other dishonest means to take money, property, or a legal right from another person.

freehold translates to "ownership" and provides the bundle of rights of ownership for an indeterminable period of time, either based upon someone's lifetime or forever. Freehold estates may either be **Fee Simple Estates** or **Life Estates.**

fructus industriales (or **emblements)** include fruit, vegetables, nuts, grasses, grains and other annually cultivated crops. These are considered personal property.

functional depreciation is a loss in value because the property is out of style for the market place, or features of the property, although working properly, are inadequate for the property

funding fee is the up-front fee the VA charges the veteran buyer at close of escrow, but normally the veteran elects to roll the funding fee into the loan

general agency is a form of agency created in a general agency agreement, normally in writing, and often referred to as a **limited power of attorney** or a **general power of attorney**. A general agent has the authority to negotiate contracts and to bind the client to a contract, but only within specially designated and limited areas.

general lien is filed in order to collect on a judgment and creates a *general lien* against all of the property the judgment debtor owns in the jurisdiction

general partnership is a form of business ownership for profit. There is only one class of partners – general partners who have unlimited liability and participate in the decision-making process of the business.

general partner are members of a general partnership and may own equal or unequal ownership positions; however, all general partners are jointly and severally liable for the debts of the partnership

general warranty deed (also known as a **warranty deed**, or **grant, bargain, and sale deed**) is the most commonly used form of deed and it contains five (5) warranties (covenants)

good faith estimate of closing costs must be provided by the lender to the borrower within 3 business days from loan application reflecting the lender's best estimate of the loan and title costs associated with the closing. This is a requirement of RESPA.

good faith suggests that the licensee must always act in the client's best interests and carry out the principal's legal instructions within the scope of the authority provided by the principal

Government National Mortgage Association (GNMA "Ginnie Mae") provides a **mortgage backed security** which was completely backed by the "full faith and credit" of the United States government. This investment instrument allowed global investment capital to be funneled into the American housing market.

graduated lease is a lease where the tenant and the landlord have agreed that with the passage of time, the leased space will become more valuable and that the tenant's lease payment should increase. The lease provides the dates on which the tenant's lease payment will increase and the amount of the increase.

graduated payment mortgage is most often seen when interest rates are high and/or the borrower is not able to qualify at the higher interest rate. The lender makes the loan with a provision that the starting payments are lower than what would otherwise be required to pay the principal and interest on the loan. The borrower agrees to increase the payment amount each year for the next two or three years until reaching the required payment. During this time, the unpaid interest is added to the unpaid balance (*negative amortization*). This will result in an increase in the size of the loan balance until the agreed increase in payment is sufficient to amortize the loan.

grandfathering allows a non-conforming use to continue as the property's use existed before the zoning was put into effect

grant, bargain, and sale deed (also known as a *warranty deed,* or *general warranty deed*) is the most commonly used form of deed and it contains five (5) warranties (covenants)

grantee is the person to whom the conveyance is made through a deed

granting clause is found in a deed and states the nature and extent of the interest conveyed – *fee simple interest in . . . ,* or *25% interest in . . . ,* etc.

grantor is the person making the conveyance by a deed to the *grantee*

gross lease is a type of lease where the tenant pays a fixed monthly rent and from those funds, the landlord pays the operating expenses of the property. This is most common in residential and small office leases.

gross rent multiplier (GRM) and *gross income multiplier (GIM),* are two alternate methods for assessing the value of income producing properties from a single family home to an industrial property. The GRM is used on smaller, residential property while the GIM is used on income producing real estate on a grander scale.

gross scheduled income, or **potential gross income**, reflects the income the property *should have earned* had there not been vacancies or bad debts and before the operating expenses were calculated

ground lease is a lease of only the land where the tenant pays for and owns any improvements including buildings. This type of lease is commonly 99 years or a very long term.

group boycotting occurs when several businesses get together and agree to withhold their patronage or not use a particular organization, possibly an escrow company, or home warranty company, or lender

habendum clause may be included in the deed (not usually required) which says "to have and to hold from this day forward"

health codes provide for minimum standards regarding a wide variety of matters, ranging from food handling and preparation standards, to general sanitation standards, to various forms of signage like "Wash Your Hands Before Returning to Work," and other similar matters

highest and best use is the most profitable legal use for the property

home equity lines of credit (HELOC), also called "equity loans," may be done when the homeowner has a substantial amount of equity in the property and wishes to use that equity (by borrowing against it) for some other purpose. These loans are sometimes called **open end mortgages** as the loan is considered "open ended" for future advances from the lender usually to a pre-determined amount.

Homestead laws protect a homeowner's personal residence from certain creditors. The exemption offers virtually absolute protection from forced sale to meet the demands of creditors, except under special circumstances. By filing the homestead exemption in some states, property owners receive a reduction from the assessed value in the calculation of property taxes.

Housing for Older Persons Act (1995) outlines the requirements *for the persons who are 55 years of age or older* exemption established in the Fair Housing Act. This exemption applies to the familial status provisions of the Fair Housing Act, but does not exempt the housing from the other provisions of the law. This law states that communities can legally market themselves as "age-restricted" or "age-qualified," provided that 80 percent of the occupied units are occupied by at least one person who is 55 years of age or older.

HUD 1, also referred to as the **Uniform Settlement Statement** must be used for the closing according to RESPA. This is an easy to read form which details the amount of the closing costs and who is paying them.

hypothecation is the pledging of property as security for a debt but retaining possession and use of the property so long as the debt is being performed as agreed. Hypothecation is the most common form of secured lending arrangements.

implied means the actions of the parties demonstrate their intent. It looks like a contracting has occurred by the appearance of things (**ostensible**).

implied agency occurs when the parties involved "act like" or "imply" that an agreement has been reached. Once this occurs, an implied agency agreement has been created, though this may have been done accidentally, inadvertently, or unintentionally.

impossibility suggests that if it is truly impossible for the parties to perform, the contract will be terminated by impossibility

impound accounts, also called *escrow accounts*, are established to hold funds for the future payment of the borrower's property taxes and casualty insurance

income approach is based upon the value of an income producing property being a reflection of the investor's required rate of return by investing in real estate. This method is most commonly utilized to determine the value of an income producing property.

*increasing and decreasing return*s takes a look at whether or not the cost of making an improvement or repair adds more to the value than making the improvement or repair costs. If it does not, then the improvement or repair should not be made, unless the owner is doing it for reasons other than increasing the value of the property.

incurable depreciation/obsolescence dictates that the loss in value is either unfixable or not cost effective to make the repairs

independent contractor status is a tax status. The Internal Revenue Service (IRS) has agreed to allow real estate professionals to elect independent contractor status for tax purposes, even though they may legally be employees. In order to qualify for this treatment, agents must have a written employment agreement with the broker which states an agent will be treated as an independent contractor for tax purposes. As an independent contractor, agents are able to deduct those reasonable and necessary business expenses. This tax treatment often offers greater deductibility of operating expenses than if taxed as an employee.

index is the cost of funds indicator used by the lender. This may be the prime rate, the T-Bill rate, the 10-year treasury bond rate, the 11th district federal reserve funds rate, the London Interbank Offering Rate (LIBOR), or any other gauge or benchmark the lender and borrower choose. As the index rises or decreases, the interest rate will adjust accordingly.

indexed lease is one where the landlord ties the lease payment to an index for inflation, such as the Consumer Price Index (CPI), and as the index increases annually, so will the tenant's lease payment

industrial real estate includes industrial parks or lands

informed parties means there can be no fraud, no misrepresentation, and no duress. The parties are fully informed, aware of the conditions of the agreement, and consent to the terms.

ingress (entrance) to the public way

interest is the compensation paid by the borrower to the lender for the period during which the borrower has use of the lender's money

interval represents the frequency in which the interest paid by the borrower will change. Most ARMS have six month or one year intervals. The interval will be stated in the note and will not be changed to another period for the life of the loan.

intestate describes those who died without a will

involuntary alienation transfers are transfers by will upon death, foreclosure, adverse possession, condemnation, and erosion or avulsion (wearing away of the land) *joint tenancy* could exist with two or more natural owners. The owners have four *unities of title: e*qual right of access and possession, equal interests, acquired their title all at the same time, and acquired their title all in the same document (PITT).

judicial partition is a means of partition ordered by a court that may either declare a portion of the property to be owned separately by the partitioning party, or by a court-ordered sale where the property is ordered sold and the proceeds distributed based on the various percentages of ownership

land is defined as the surface of the earth, extending upward to infinity and downward to the center of the earth. It includes all things that are attached to the surface of the earth, like trees and shrubs, and the water that exists on and below the land. Land also includes the soil and minerals below the surface (termed the *subsurface*) and the air above the earth's surface (termed the *airspace*).

land contract, also called a *contract for deed,* is a form of seller financing. The *vendor* (seller) retains *legal title* to the property but transfers *equitable title* to the *vendee* (buyer). If the buyer does perform as required, then at the conclusion of performance, the seller is obligated to convey legal title to the buyer where it will join with the equitable title the buyer already holds.

latent defects are those defects that are not visible. These may be known or unknown to the seller or agent. If these are known, both the seller and the agent have a responsibility to reveal them.

law of decreasing returns means that the cost of making an improvement will NOT be covered by the added value to the property (*incurable*)

law of increasing returns means that the cost of making an improvement will be more than covered by the added value to the property (**curable**)

law/statute of descent and distribution applies when a person dies intestate. The state in which the property is located has laws to ensure that the real and personal property transfer to the decedent's heirs according to the state's formula. Essentially, the state is making a will for the decedent.

lead is found in plumbing pipes in older homes. Lead-based solder and lead-based seals could, over time, place harmful quantities of lead in the water.

lead-based paint can be found in homes built prior to 1978. Discovery was made that lead-based paint was often eaten by small children as they chewed on cabinet doors and trim. Lead-based paint, if ingested, can result in brain damage and death.

leaking underground storage tanks (LUST) are found in older gas stations and other facilities where gasoline and other petroleum products were stored in steel or iron underground tanks. The primary hazard is leaking and the contamination of ground water as the petroleum product leaches further into the soil.

lease option agreements start out as leases, but include an *option to purchase* by the expiration of the leasehold. The price and terms are negotiated up front.

lease purchase agreements start out as leases but include a *purchase agreement* that will go into effect by the expiration of the leasehold. The price and terms are negotiated up front.

leased fee means the landlord still owns the property, but has surrendered the rights of possession and use to the tenant

leasehold improvements are improvements or alterations to the leased space. Normally they are done at the *landlord's expense* and remain a part of the leased space as the landlord's property when the tenant vacates.

leasehold interest refers to the tenant's rights to the leased property, providing the right to possess and use the property

legacy **is** money given through a will

legal descriptions describe one parcel of property so well that it cannot be confused with another parcel

legal title is secured when the closing is completed, the deed transfers title from the seller to the buyer, and the deed is recorded

legality of object means the purpose underlying the contract must be legal

lessee is a party to a lease agreement and is the tenant

lessor is a party to a lease agreement and is the owner/landlord

license is the giving of permission by the landowner to allow another to come upon the land for specific purposes. The license is a privilege and is revocable.

lien theory states the ***mortgagor*** (borrower) retains legal and equitable title. The ***mortgagee*** (lender) has only a lien on the property as security for the debt. In order for the lender to take the property for sale, foreclosure proceedings must be initiated to obtain the legal title.

life estates are based upon the life of the owner or some other designated person. Life estates are not inheritable so it is necessary to pre-determine to whom title shall pass upon the passing of the named party.

limited liability company (LLC) is a business structure that is a hybrid of a corporation and a limited partnership

limited partnerships must have at least one general partner, and there may be any number of *limited partners*. The general partners have the right to full participation in the activities of the partnership and are individually liable for the obligations and debts of the partnership. Limited partners have limited liability and do not partake in operating the business.

liquidated damages are those damages the contract pre-addressed that may be received in the event of default

lis pendens is placed in the public records and gives notice that litigation is pending concerning the property. Lis pendens tend to prevent the property from being sold before the dispute is resolved.

listing agreement is an employment contract between the seller of property and the real estate broker. It is important to note the contract is between the seller and the broker; not the salesperson.

littoral rights describe the rights of owners whose land borders large (commercially navigable) lakes, seas, and oceans

loan originators are those persons or businesses who *actually make* the loans in the primary market

loan to value ratio (LTV) is the ratio between the loan being made and the appraised value of the property given as collateral, or the purchase price, *whichever is less*

lot, block, and subdivision legal description involves the surveying of a plot of land and then divided into blocks and lots, streets, access roads, utility easements, parks, etc. Then, the blocks and lots are assigned numbers and letters. The resultant drawing is called a *plat map* or *subdivision plat*.

margin represents the *profit and overhead* the lender wants to earn above the costs of funds. This will be stated in the note and will not be changed to another amount for the life of the loan. The margin is added to the index to calculate the interest rate.

market analysis is prepared by the real estate professional using the data in the *local Multiple Listing Service™* to estimate the value by examining sold listings, active listings, expired listings, and days on market.

market data or comparable sales approach is the most common particularly for residential properties. The appraiser looks for properties which have sold recently, in close proximity, and comparable in features and amenities to the subject property.

market value is the value of property today based on a probable price a seller would be willing to sell and a buyer would be willing to pay under normal conditions

marketable title means "good" title; good enough for an attorney to recommend the buyer accept

master plan allows each local government to develop a master plan for the community. The master plan should take into consideration the needs of the community, the location of various uses of land, the potential for conflict between uses, and the orderly growth of the community.

master planned communities develop plans that include recreation centers, parks, playgrounds, and other amenities, as well as reserved spaces for schools, churches, retail establishments, and other facilities. Many master planned communities are gated, so as to restrict access to residents.

material fact is a fact that would be important to a reasonable person in deciding whether to engage or not to engage in a particular transaction; or would affect the price paid. It is an important fact as distinguished from some unimportant or trivial detail.

mechanic's lien protects those persons who provide labor or materials to improve another's property. This lien is effective as of the date of first work or first delivery of materials, not the date it is filed in the public records.

metes and bounds legal description relies on a description of *metes* (distance and direction) and *bounds* (landmarks or boundary edges) to define the borders of a parcel of land. A metes-and-bounds description uses a *point of beginning (POB)*, and then directions and linear measurements to define the borders of the property, finally returning to the POB.

mill is one-tenth of a penny or $1/1000^{th}$ of a dollar

misrepresentation can be negligent statements or just plain mistakes, and are considered "innocent" in nature. *Negligent misrepresentations* occur when a broker or agent should have known that a statement about a material fact was false. The broker's lack of awareness of the fact is no excuse. Also, the concept of negligent misrepresentation extends to situations where the broker or agent simply fails to do something or follow through as expected.

mixed use projects are uses of property that are different such as residential, retail, restaurant, office and medical/dental facilities

mold is a fungi that thrives on moisture. While some molds are benign or even beneficial, others can cause allergic reactions when inhaled or touched.

monetary encumbrance is a lien giving another the right to repossess or foreclose against real or personal property and to sell the property to pay that debt or obligation owed to the lienholder

mortgage bankers work as a "middle man" between mortgage brokers and the ultimate investors. Some mortgage bankers have funds of their own with which to fund the loan, but will normally then sell the loans they have created to liquidate capital to lend again. A significant difference between a mortgage banker and a mortgage broker is that bankers often *do* provide servicing for the loans after they are made. They service their own loans and provide this service for investors at an additional charge.

mortgage brokers are the *loan originators* most common in the market. The mortgage broker takes the application for the loan from the borrower, then "shops" the loan to find an investor who will make the loan and who will offer competitive terms. If a loan is made, the mortgage broker is paid a fee for services. Mortgage brokers do not provide loan servicing for the investor which would include collecting the loan payments, accounting tasks, handling escrow accounts for future payment of insurance, property taxes, etc. Once the loan is closed and funded, the job of the mortgage broker is essentially done.

Mortgage Insurance Premium (MIP) is paid by the borrower both in an up-front payment and also monthly for the life of the FHA loan. The amount, or percentage, for these two costs changes from time to time.

mortgage is a contract which creates a *monetary lien* against real property. Mortgages are most frequently used in the states east of the Rocky Mountains.   Some think of mortgages as the "what if?" document where the question "what if the borrower stops making payments?" is addressed.

mortgagee is the lender who receives the mortgage from the borrower in exchange for the lender providing the financing

mortgagor is the borrower; the one giving the mortgage in exchange for receiving the loan

Multiple Listing Service (MLS)™ is available to members of the local association of REALTORS® in order to access data on member broker listings

multiple-party representation is another term for dual agency

mutual agreement or *mutual consent* to terminate a contract is where the parties decide they do not want to go forward and mutually agree that each should be released from the contract. By mutual agreement, the contract is terminated.

naked title is "bare" legal but with none of the benefits of ownership. This concept applies in a deed of trust where the trustee holds naked title and the beneficiary holds equitable title.

National Association of REALTORS® (NAR) is an organization, which has state-level and local associations under its national umbrella, and promotes a higher level of professionalism, integrity, and education than non-members

National Do Not Call Registry and federal legislation allows for consumers to add their phone numbers to a list managed by the Federal Trade Commission (FTC).   Real estate agents may not call anyone on this list. Several exceptions should be noted.

natural person is a human being

negative amortization occurs when the unpaid interest is added to the unpaid balance. This will result in an increase in the size of the loan balance until the agreed increase in payment is sufficient to amortize the loan.

negotiable instrument refers to the promissory note meaning the lender may sell the note without consent from the borrower in order to liquidate the lender's funds

net lease is a lease where the tenant pays a *base rent* (fixed monthly rent) and in addition to the base rent, pays some, or all of the operating expenses of the property

net listing is a commission arrangement and is not permitted in many states as the arrangement inherently creates a conflict of interest between the broker and the client. In this situation, the broker's commission is anything in excess of the seller's desired net proceeds, payoff of liens, and closing costs.

net operating income is the gross scheduled income of the property minus the property's annual operating expenses and also minus the annual vacancies and bad debts the property experiences

non-conforming use (NCU) happens when a property is put to a given use where there are no zoning ordinances or zoning allowing it otherwise. Time passes and now the use does not "conform" with the current zoning.

non-natural person can be a corporation, a limited liability company (LLC), a partnership, or a limited partnership

note, or **promissory note,** is a legal document which creates and identifies the debt. The note is a contract and the equivalent of an I.O.U. It is the document which creates the debt between the borrower and the lender. It is the *evidence of the debt*.

novation is the substitution of a new *contract* for an old one

novation of parties is where a new *party* is substituted for an existing party

obsolescence is another term for depreciation; a loss in value

offer and acceptance is sometimes referred to as "mutual assent." This essential element of a contract shows there is a "meeting of the minds," that an offer was made and acceptance of that offer was reached.

offer is a proposed contract made by the offeror. Note that an offer becomes a contract when the offer has been accepted by the offeree and communication of that acceptance has been received by the offeror.

offeree is the party *receiving* the offer

offeror is the party *making* the offer

open listing is a listing contract whereby the seller agrees to pay a commission to *any* broker who procures a ready, willing, and able buyer at list price and terms, or such other price and terms agreeable to the seller. The seller gives *no exclusivity* to the broker, and the seller may sell the property himself without owing a commission to any broker. The seller may also have several open listings in effect.

operating expenses are costs associated with operating the building such as utilities, taxes, management fees, etc. and should not be confused with "debt service fees" which are incurred as a result of financing the original purchase of the property. When expressed as a percentage, they express a percentage of the effective/adjusted gross income.

operation of law refers to the fact that some contracts could be terminated by the courts or statutory prohibition

opinion of title is prepared by an attorney after reviewing the abstract of title and will render an opinion as to whether the title is *marketable* (good)

option contracts are between the owner of the property, the *optionor*, and a purchaser, *optionee,* who wants to have a period of time in which to decide on the purchase of the property. This is a unilateral contract in that the optionor has no obligation to perform until and unless the optionee decides to purchase. At that time, the optionor would complete the sale of the property to the optionee. The optionee must offer *option money*, better described as the agreed valuable consideration, in exchange for the option to purchase or not to purchase.

ordinary life estate calls for the title to the property to pass upon the death of the owner

ostensible **means** the actions of the parties demonstrate their intent. It looks like a contracting has occurred by the appearance of things (*implied*).

package mortgage provides financing for both the real estate and the personal property that goes with it. Common examples are loans that cover major appliances like refrigerators, washers and dryers, window treatments, equipment, furniture, etc. that are all included in the purchase price.

Parol Evidence Rule states that verbal words and representations will not be binding nor overrule any written agreements

partial release clause, found in a blanket mortgage, allows the builder to pull the parcel sold "out from under" the blanket mortgage

partition means to divide out an interest where there are multiple owners

patent defects (an archaic term, but still used in construction), are accessible, un-hidden, visible defects

percentage lease exists when the tenant pays a *base rent* plus a percentage of the gross business income, normally less any payment for returned goods. The philosophy is the landlord's location, anchor tenants, and marketing contributes to the overall business income of the tenant. This lease may be gross or net.

performance is the most desirable outcome of a contract. The parties perform all of their duties and receive all of their rights as agreed.

personal property is defined as all property which can be owned by an owner but does not fit the definition of real property. One important definitional difference is that personal property can be moved.

physical depreciation is a loss in value because the property is in a bad state of repair, or some of the components of the property are nearly worn out

physical partition is a means of partition done by agreement of the owners where a legal description for the agreed upon portion of the property is created and deeded out to the partitioning party by the remainder of the owners

Planned Unit Development (PUD) **is** a combination of housing, recreational amenities, and commercial uses all in one "planned development"

plat map (or ***subdivision plat***) is used in the lot, block, and subdivision legal description method. The map shows the subdivision location and the boundaries of all individual lots.

plottage and assemblage comes into play when several smaller parcels are assembled into one large parcel, often resulting in the larger parcel having a greater value than the sum of the values of the individual smaller parcels. This increase in value is called p***lottage*** and the act of bringing the parcels together is called a***ssemblage***.

point equals 1% of the loan amount. The IRS considers a point to be a form of interest paid upfront instead of over the term of the loan. Discount points are charged when there is a cost to receive a certain rate or to buy a rate down ("discount").

point of beginning (POB) is the starting point and the ending point in a metes and bounds legal description

police powers represents the government's right to regulate for the benefit of the general health and welfare of its citizens. Traditionally, police powers describe those activities of the state which regulate real estate such as the enacting of zoning regulations, building codes, health and safety regulations, traffic laws, and family law.

potential gross income, or **gross scheduled income,** reflects the income the property *should have earned* had there not been vacancies or bad debts and before the operating expenses were calculated

pre-approval demonstrates the borrower's ability to qualify subject to conditions being satisfied. Often done in the form of a pre-approval letter, this document strengthens the buyer's position as the buyer negotiates a purchase agreement with the seller.

prepayment clause informs the borrower under what circumstances the lender will accept payment, in whole or in part, before the due date. In some cases, the lender is happy to have the loan paid off sooner than planned such as when opportunities exist to use the capital at a higher yield. But should the lender not want the loan prepaid, such as when such opportunities do not exist, the issue will be addressed in the prepayment clause.

prepayment penalties are financial penalties assessed against the borrower and associated with loans that are paid off early, before the end of the term

pre-qualification is an interview, in person or by phone, between the lender and the borrower. The lender will typically obtain consent and run a credit report to look for red flags. Calculations as to debt to income ratios and debt to housing expense ratios are done.

price per front foot is a method to determine value, similar to the price per square foot method. Whenever land dimensions are given, the *first* dimension is always the front footage – that border of the property which is adjacent to the road frontage.

price per square foot is useful in determining a property's fair market value. Looking at your comparables, divide the sale price by the living area square footage for each comp, and calculate an average price per square foot. Then, apply that figure to the square footage in the subject property.

price-fixing is the act of agreeing to set prices or fees at a predefined level, as opposed to allowing markets and market forces to set them. This is illegal. Real estate brokers must independently set commission rates for their own companies, and they must never discuss these with other brokers in an attempt to arrive at a standard fee.

primary market represents those persons or businesses who *actually make* the loans. This primary market is often called the *loan originators*.

prime rate is the interest rate charged by banks to their most creditworthy customers (usually the most prominent and stable business customers)

principal delegates authority to the agent to represent the principal's interests in a transaction. The principal is obligated by contract to compensate the agent and not hinder the agent's ability to fulfill the agent's fiduciary obligations. Another definition of ***principal*** pertains to financing where the principal portion of the payment reduces the loan balance.

principal meridians are the primary vertical lines referenced when using the U.S. Government Rectangular Survey system
prior appropriation means that someone, often the government, has *already taken* and reserved the water rights for themselves and can sell or lease those rights separately

priority refers to the order in which liens were recorded. The priority of liens will determine which lien gets paid off first, then second, etc. in the event of a foreclosure. Note that tax liens also take a first priority position regardless of the date of recording.

private mortgage insurance was created to encourage lenders to lend at loan-to-value ratios above 80%. Given that a lender would loan only 80% without any further assurances, "PMI" provides insurance against loss on that portion of the loan above 80%.

probate is a formal judicial process that ensures that assets are distributed properly. Probate accomplishes three things: confirms that a particular will is valid if there is a will, adds up or accounts for all of a decedent's assets, and identifies the people who will receive the assets.

processing is performed by the processors who will verify all information provided to the loan officer, order the appraisal as well as title documentation, flood certifications, insurance, verify employment and asset account information, obtain any missing documentation, and lock the rate prior to underwriting

procuring cause means to be the cause of the chain of events that caused the sale

profits are the giving of permission by the landowner to allow another to come onto the land for the limited purpose of removing crops, timber, soil, etc. Here the person receiving *profits* is neither a trespasser, nor a license holder, and has no easement. He is there for a very limited purpose which can be revoked at any time.

progression implies if a property is significantly poorer than surrounding properties, the surrounding properties will tend to cause the subject property's value to **progress** upward as a result of the higher value of the surrounding properties

promissory note is a legal document which creates and identifies the debt. The **note** is a contract and the equivalent of an I.O.U. It is the document which creates the debt between the borrower and the lender. It is the *evidence of the debt*.

property management agreement is a contract between the owner and a broker/property manager which should specify both the owner's and the property manager's duties, responsibilities, and under what conditions the property manager has the authority to make decisions or sign a contract

property management means to handle the management of the owner's income property, maximizing the owner's return on investment while also protecting the value of the property itself. Many owners do not wish to take on the day-to-day activities and hassles associated with being a landlord and hire property managers to perform those functions on the owner's behalf.

property tax is a state tax, collected locally, based upon the assessed value of the real estate (land + improvements)

proprietary lease is utilized in a cooperative and gives each owner of the corporation a lease to occupy his or her unit

prospecting is the marketing of yourself in order to attract real estate clients to doing business with you

public land use controls include environmental protection laws, subdivision regulations, and zoning

puffing or **puffery** is the exaggeration of a property's benefits such as "This home has the best curb appeal on the block." Puffing is legal because it is based on individual opinions, but agents must make sure that none of their comments or statements about real estate can be treated as fraudulent.

punitive damages go above and beyond liquidated damages and may be sought to "punish" the breaching party and compensate the injured party

pur autre vie, translates to "for another's life." This life estate dictates that title to the property, that the life tenant enjoys, shall transfer to another individual upon the death of some other named person.

purchase money mortgage is any portion of the purchase price which the seller "carries" (finances). In real estate, the owner of the property being sold may be in the position to act as the lender.

quit claim deed offers no warranties at all. The grantor is *quitting* any claim the grantor may have to the property, but does not assert that there is any claim at all. This deed is often used to remove liens and encumbrances from title, to surrender community property claims, or to clear *clouds on the title.*

radon is an odorless, colorless, radioactive gas produced naturally by the radioactive materials in the ground. It represents another environmental hazard and has been linked to lung cancer.

range lines are imaginary lines vertically parallel to the principal meridians when using the U.S. Government Rectangular Survey system *ranges* are strips of land, 6 miles apart, running vertically parallel to the principal meridian when using the U.S. Government Rectangular Survey system

real estate is defined as the land, plus all *improvements*, which are the man-made artificial things attached to the land. Notice the term *artificial* describes the man-made things that we know as buildings, fences, driveways, swimming pools, etc.

Real Estate Settlement Procedures Act (RESPA) requires lenders to inform the parties to a covered real estate transaction what the closing costs and charges are, and which costs they pay for

real property consists of physical land, the natural features, the man-made improvements to the land, and, the bundle of rights of ownership of real property.

REALTOR® is a member of the professional organization the *National Association of REALTORS® (NAR)*. Note the word REALTOR® is always put in all capital letters followed by the registered trademark symbol. Also note REALTOR® is pronounced "REAL-TOR®" (real tore) and not "REAL-A-TOR®" (real a ter).

reconciliation uses a "weighted average" giving the appraiser a method of expressing confidence in the results given by the application of the various approaches. It boils the three values derived from the three approaches down to one final number.

recording fees represent a state established charge for the recording of documents in the public records of the county

recording is the filing of important documents with the county recorder's office thus providing ***actual notice***

redlining is the illegal act by a lender who refuses to lend in an area because it is populated with members of a protected class

regression implies if a property is significantly better than surrounding properties, its value will **regress** downward toward the value of the surrounding properties

Regulation Z requires lenders to disclose true costs of obtaining credit

rejection of offer simply says "no," and by doing so, has rejected the last offer, without counteroffering. An offeree should be aware that a rejection does not obligate the offeror to do anything whatsoever.
religion, national origin, marital status, or source of income.

remainderman will take the title to the property as a fee simple estate upon the death of the life tenant

replacement cost represents the theoretical building of a substantially similar property, using currently available materials and construction techniques

reproduction cost would be used if the building were so unique that using available materials and techniques would not produce a substantially similar building

rescission occurs when either party decides to call off the contract and return the earnest money deposit to the buyer. This is a complete reversal of the contract, putting everyone back to where they were before the contract.

reserve requirements fluctuate should the Federal Reserve determine that the amount of available money in the system is either creating inflationary pressures on the economy, or is insufficient to sustain desired economic growth, reserve requirements may be adjusted.

residential real estate is usually defined as four or fewer residential units

reverse annuity mortgage (RAM) *is* designed mainly for older homeowners who own their homes free and clear, or who have very large equities, but who do not wish to sell or cash out the equity in their homes in one lump sum. The RAM lender will pay to the RAM borrower an agreed upon sum each month. In effect, the RAM borrower is drawing out equity in the home monthly.

reversionary interest belongs to the person to whom the property will revert (the original owner) in a life estate

revocation is a legal remedy available to the seller when the buyer defaults. The seller *revokes* the contact and *retains* the earnest money deposit.

right of first refusal is a scenario where the holder of the right of first refusal has the right to match any offer made on a property

right of survivorship means that upon the death of one of the joint tenants, the share of the deceased joint tenant is divided equally among all of the *surviving* joint tenants

riparian rights are common-law rights granted to owners along the course of a river or stream

rule of reason places an obligation on all of us to conduct ourselves as the "reasonable person" would, and to always act in a reasonable fashion. Ultimately, it is often the judge or jury who tells us, after the fact, if our conduct was reasonable.

sale leaseback is an arrangement whereby the buyer and seller agree to a leasehold, the seller remains in possession of the sold property under agreed upon lease terms, and compensates the buyer for that possession. This is ideal for an investor who is purchasing the property as an income producing property as the seller becomes the tenant.

satisfaction of mortgage is issued by the lender indicating the loan has been paid in full

scarcity is the extent to which the supply in the marketplace will have an influence on the value. If there are vast numbers of similar properties, any one property's value is greatly diminished. Likewise, if there are few or no such properties, the value will increase.

secondary liability comes into play under an assignment of a contract. When one party desires to assign his rights, obligations, and benefits under the contract to a third party, he may generally do so, however that original party will remain "secondarily liable" for performance and obligations should the third party fail to perform.

secondary market represents those persons or businesses who actually *fund* the loan. This group is where the *lenders* go to get the funds to lend.

sections are described when using the U.S. Government Rectangular Survey system. There are 36 sections in a township. Each section measures 5,280 feet on a side (one mile) and contains 640 acres of land.

separate property is property owned by an individual prior to a marriage or acquired after the marriage by gift or by inheritance. It remains the sole and separate property of the party owning it.

services of real estate brokerage are commonly described as buying, selling, leasing, exchanging, negotiating, offering, auctioning, and appraising for another person, for compensation. If an individual is performing any of these services of real estate, for compensation, or even for the expectation of being compensated, a real estate license from the state where the property is located is required.

servient tenement serves the dominant tenement allowing the dominant tenement the right of passage

setback is the required distance between structures

settlement is another term for the closing of a real estate transaction

Sherman Antitrust Act is among the federal laws pertaining to antitrust legislation. Violations of this act can range to $1 million for individuals and $100 million for corporations.

short sale of a property occurs when a property is sold for less than loan balances owed

single agency is the typical, agency relationship used in real estate. One agent represents the seller and another agent represents the buyer, in most cases. Every client who enters into an agency agreement with a broker has the right to know that in a single transaction, the agent exclusively represents only his side of a transaction.

special agency is a form of agency most often used in real estate. Special agency is created in an agreement, often in writing. The special agent represents the client and has all of the fiduciary duties, but has no authority to bind the client to anything. The role of the special agent is simply to represent the interests of the client, but the special agent must allow the client to make the final decision whether or not to be contractually bound.

special assessments are levied against properties for special improvements, such as sidewalks, street lights, landscaping of public areas, and other such improvements. The special assessment is charged against the properties which *directly benefit* from the improvements.

special warranty deed is used by executors, trustees and universal or general agents of the grantor. The only warranty created with the special warranty deed is the *warranty against undisclosed encumbrances*.

speculative homes ("spec homes") are new homes where the builder "speculates" what the market will do by completing a small number of homes without buyers under contract

sphere of influence is all the people you know and an excellent source of business

spot zoning represents the zoning authority's decision to rezone a small area in a zone different from the surrounding parcels

Statute of Frauds requires all real estate contracts, except short-term leases (less than 1 year), to be in writing. All other contracts where the amount in controversy exceeds $500 must also be in writing to be enforceable.   "Enforceable" means a dispute between the parties will be heard in court and a judge will "enforce" the provisions of the contract.

Statute of Limitations is a legal limit to the time frame under which the injured party can legally sue the breaching party and this limit varies from state to state

steering is the illegal showing of properties to a prospective buyer or tenant only in areas of the market which are predominantly of the same ethnicity as the prospect

stigmatized property is a term that applies when a property become "defamed" because of some event that has occurred at the property or nearby, or because of the presence of some negative factor in the local area

straight loan, (also called a **term loan** or an **interest only loan**) is a scenario where the borrower pays only interest during the life of the loan. At the end of term, the entire principal balance is paid off in full. There is no amortization.

subagent is a person to whom agency has been delegated, always by an agent who is responsible to a principal and always with the permission of the principal. Subagents assist in carrying out client-based functions on behalf of the principal. Note that subagents from the same company have the same fiduciary duties and responsibilities as the original agent.

subdivision plat (or **plat map)** is used in the lot, block, and subdivision legal description method. It is required by most municipalities of a developer, who wishes to subdivide the large parcel into lots. The map clearly identifies the "lay of the land" identifying individual parcels, lot sizes, streets, utilities, and other information as required for approval.

subdivision regulations contain regulations such as street widths, provisions for sidewalks and street lights, drainage provisions, lot size, house size, house styles, roof material, exterior finishes, and a host of other matters required for the specific subdivision

subject property is the property for which the value is being appraised

subject to has two applications in real estate. In a wrap-around mortgage, the buyer purchases the property from the seller "subject to" the existing mortgage but does not assume personal liability for it. The other application is synonymous with **contingency.**

subordination agreement is an agreement between two lien holders to swap priority position

substitution and the **principle of substitution** is based on the likelihood that the market will not pay substantially more for one property over another if the properties are substantially the same

suit for damages is a legal remedy to either party for breach of contract on the part of the other party. A suit for damages will require the defaulting party to pay the other for any actual costs associated with the hardship.

suit for specific performance is a legal action which will require the defaulting party to perform all duties as specified in the contract

suit to quiet title is a court action taken if it is discovered there is a gap in title and will often involve the use of a **quit claim deed**

Superfund Amendment and Reauthorization Act (1986), SARA, clarified regulations regarding hazardous waste and limited liability for some parties, including innocent landowners and real estate brokers

supply and demand affects the value of the subject property. High Demand + Low Supply = Higher Values. Low Demand + High Supply = Lower Values.

survey is a study performed by a surveyor which determines property boundary lines. A survey will also uncover any violations of setbacks or encroachments.

tenancy by the entireties has the four unities of title found in joint tenancy, with the additional requirement that the parties *must be married*. Thus, there would be only two parties in a tenancy by the entireties situation but are treated as one legal person.

tenant in severalty exists when there is only one owner. The title to the property has been "severed" from all others. This form of ownership is available to natural and non-natural persons.

tenants in common could exist when there are two or more owners. There is only one **unity of title**, the right of equal access and possession.

term loan, (also called a "straight loan" or an **interest only loan**) is a scenario where the borrower pays only interest during the life of the loan. At the end of term, the entire principal balance is paid off in full. There is no amortization.

testate describes those individuals who have died with a will. They are said to have died testate.

testator is the person who made the will and died testate

tie-in agreements involve agreements to sell customers one product or service only if they purchase another product. Usually the sale of a desirable product is tied into the purchase of a less desirable product.

tiers are strips of land, 6 miles apart, running horizontally parallel to the base line when using the U.S. Government Rectangular Survey system

time is of the essence simply put, means that if a specific time period is set out in the contract, in which one of the parties is to do something, and has not done it when the allotted period of time expires, the other party may declare a breach

timeshare is the right to use and occupy a residential unit on a periodic recurring basis, according to an arrangement among the other owners. In most timeshare projects, the timeshare buyer purchases a right to use a unit (the actual room or suite where the persons will stay) for a week.

title is synonymous with *ownership* of real property. It means *ownership* of real property and includes the bundle of rights plus a **deed** to the land which serves as evidence of ownership.

title theory states the **mortgagor** (borrower) gives the **mortgagee** (lender) **legal title** and retains **equitable title**. Legal title is returned to the mortgagor upon full payment of the debt.

townhomes may appear to be single family dwellings which are physically attached to adjacent structures. Each townhome is usually two-or three stories and typically sits on its own parcel of land. The owner of the townhome owns the land upon which the structure sits and also owns other common property (pools, tennis courts, parks, etc.) in the townhome project as a tenant in common with the other owners in the development.

township lines are imaginary lines horizontally parallel to the base lines when using the U.S. Government Rectangular Survey system

townships are formed by the intersection of the ranges and tiers when using the U.S. Government Rectangular Survey system. Each township contains 36 sections.

tract homes are built in a subdivision which typically has a few models from which purchasers can choose to have the builder construct on their behalf

trade fixtures are generally items of personal property that are installed in such a fashion as to make them a fairly permanent part of the leased space

transaction or transactional broker is a strategy used in some states to deal with dual agency concerns. A transaction broker is an agent without fiduciary duties but who handles the transaction from start to finish. Those states adopting the transaction broker approach take the position that the real estate professionals represent the transaction and not the parties to the transaction.

transfer taxes, sometimes referred to as *conveyance taxes*, *revenue stamps*, *documentary stamps*, or *deed stamps,* are a *state* tax, collected locally, based upon the value of real property when it is sold. It is normally paid by the seller at closing and is based upon a declaration of value.

transferability applies in that the property must be able to be sold (transferred) from one owner to another. If the property cannot be sold due to restrictions on its ownership, such as a burden on title, the property's value is greatly diminished.

trigger term is any term of the financing and "triggers" the need to disclose *all* credit terms – all or none.

trust account is another term for an ***escrow account*** established by a broker for the holding of the principal's funds until funding, such as with a buyer's earnest money deposit

trust is a device where one person transfers real property to another person for the benefit of a third, with the understanding that the real estate asset (and possibly other assets as well) will be used to care for the trustor.

trustee is an independent third party chosen by the lender and to whom the power of sale is granted in a deed of trust

trustor is the borrower in a deed of trust. The term is also used to describe the individual or business entity (e.g., a corporation, LLC, etc.) who transfers the property to the **trustee** within a trust.

U.S. Government Rectangular Survey System lays an imaginary grid of horizontal and vertical lines across the country and references the subject property within that grid

underwriting is the final review and decision making process pertaining to granting the loan

undivided interest applies when there is more than one owner to a property. The parties are said to hold *undivided interests* meaning that no owner can claim a specific physical portion of the property as belonging to that owner only. Multi-party ownership deals with *interests in* rather than *physical portions* of the property.

unenforceable contract appears to be valid, but if there is a disagreement between the parties in the performance of duties and the receipt of rights, the courts will not get involved in a resolution.

Uniform Residential Appraisal Report (URAR) is the standard format of a written appraisal as required by many institutions

Uniform Residential Landlord Tenant Act (URLTA) provisions were created to clarify, standardize, and modernize the rights and responsibilities of tenants and landlords in the United States

Uniform Settlement Statement (**HUD 1)** must be used for the closing according to RESPA. This is an easy to read form which details the amount of the closing costs and who is paying them.

Uniform Standards of Professional Appraisal Practice (USPAP) establishes the quality control standards applicable for real property, personal property, intangibles, and business valuation appraisal analysis and reports

unilateral means "one sided." Often taking the form of an option contract, a unilateral contract is binding on one party should the other party elect to perform under the agreement. It is one sided in that the party with the option does not ever have to perform.

unity of title is a condition of ownership which is common to all who hold title to the property. The more unities there are, the more the owners have in common (in their ownership) with each other. The four unities of title are time, title, interest, and possession.

universal agency is a form of agency created in a written **unlimited power of attorney** which grants the agent the authority to do anything the clients could do for themselves. Universal agency authorizes binding the client to contracts and authorizes the sale or other disposition of real and personal property.

up zoning takes place if additional uses are *added* to those already available for a property. This normally adds value to the property.

urea formaldehyde foam insulation (UFFI) has been used as an insulation in residential and commercial buildings. Ingestion and inhalation present significant health hazards.

usury refers to maximum interest rates lenders can charge on certain loans as established by the state. To the extent that the interest charged exceeds the statutory amount, it is referred to as *usurious* and cannot be collected. Not all states have such provisions.

utility implies that property must be useful in the eyes of the market. If the real estate is not useful (not good for anything) it has little or no value.

vacancies and bad debts are those losses to the gross income the owner incurred due to units being vacant for any length of time and for rents that should have been, but were not, collected. When expressed as a percentage, they reflect a percentage of the gross scheduled income.

valid contract contains visible evidence of all five essential elements of a contract (competent parties, offer and acceptance, legality of object, informed parties, and consideration) and is therefore binding and enforceable on all parties.

variance is a request for some leeway in using a parcel which violates the zoning regulations

vendee is a buyer

vendor is a seller

vesting clause states the vesting option selected by the grantee such as *in severalty,* as *a tenant in common,* as *joint tenants with right of survivorship,* etc.

Veteran's Administration (VA) guaranteed loans are not normally made by the VA. Loans are made through private lenders. The VA may fund the loan if there is no available lender. The VA does not set interest rates on VA loans. The interest is determined by the lender to be competitive in the market.

void agreement lacks any one or more of the essential elements of a contract and has no legal effect. It is not binding on the parties.

voidable contract appears to be valid but may be disaffirmed because it is missing competent parties (legal capacity) such as a minor, or is missing voluntary, informed parties such as a contract executed under misrepresentation, fraud, or duress. In a voidable contract, the party suffering the legal disability has the right to void the contract, provided it is done within a reasonable time.

voluntary alienation usually involves a deed where the owner voluntarily transfers his title to another person

warranty (or ***covenant)*** is a promise by the ***grantor*** to the ***grantee*** concerning the title to the property, that some condition exists and will continue to exist, or, that a condition does not exist and never will

warranty against undisclosed encumbrances is a covenant in a deed that claims the grantor has disclosed to the grantee all encumbrances on the property, if any

warranty deed (also known as a ***general warranty deed,*** or ***grant, bargain, and sale deed)*** is the most commonly used form of deed and it contains five warranties (covenants).

warranty of further assurances is a covenant in a deed where the grantor promises that should a claim of superior title be made, the grantor will defend against the claim and defeat it.

warranty of quiet enjoyment promises the grantee will be able to enjoy ownership of the property without hearing anyone make a valid claim of superior title or right to the property

warranty of seisin is a covenant in a deed that states the grantor owns the property and has the right and power to convey the property

warranty of title forever is a deed covenant where the grantor promises that should another party be able to establish a superior claim to the title, the grantor will pay back to the grantee the purchase price (the *money back guarantee*)

wrap around mortgage (or **all-inclusive deed of trust**) is a form of seller financing (purchase money mortgage) available only where there is no existing **due on sale** clause in the original mortgage document. The seller still owes on the original mortgage (the **underlying mortgage**) and continues to make those payments. The buyer makes payments to the seller for the new amount financed as a purchase money mortgage.

writ of attachment has the effect of preventing the transfer of assets until the lawsuit is concluded

writ of execution is utilized to assist in the collection of a judgment. The court will issue the writ of execution to the sheriff, which directs the sheriff to seize all property of the defendant in the jurisdiction, sell it, and apply the proceeds against the judgment.

zoning establishes what uses are available for each parcel of land. The categories of uses generally found in zoning ordinances are agricultural, residential, commercial, industrial, and governmental.